Original title:
The Ocean's Heart

Copyright © 2025 Creative Arts Management OÜ
All rights reserved.

Author: Atticus Thornton
ISBN HARDBACK: 978-1-80581-686-7
ISBN PAPERBACK: 978-1-80581-213-5
ISBN EBOOK: 978-1-80581-686-7

A Tale of Pearl and Stone

In the depths where the clams sing loud,
A pearl once wore a pompous shroud.
It thought it glimmered more than gold,
But a rock just yawned and joked, 'I'm bold!'

The crab found humor in its pride,
With sideways antics, it would slide.
The pearl just sighed, 'What would you know?'
The rock just laughed, 'I steal the show!'

Dances in the Halcyon Waves

The fish throw parties with bubble tunes,
While dolphins dance beneath the moons.
A clownfish twirls with a funny frown,
And a turtle rides in a polka-dot gown.

The seagulls swoop, on snacks they dive,
While starfish hum, feeling alive.
A shrimp's the DJ, spinning with glee,
In a world where everyone's carefree!

Mysteries Entwined in Seaweed

Seaweed whispers secrets, oh so sly,
'What happens at high tide, we can't deny.'
A crab disguised, just playing along,
Mistaking the seaweed for a trendy thong.

The starfish giggles at such a sight,
'These creatures sure know how to delight.'
While octopuses, with eight arms they wave,
Silly sea antics are all that they crave.

Breaths of the Surf's Caress

Each wave a tickle, a playful tease,
The seafoam giggles, as it sneezes.
With sandy toes and a joyful splash,
Even the seashells join in the bash.

Frogs in the tide pools start to croak,
While waves deliver a tide-soaked joke.
Laughter echoes across the strand,
As the ocean rolls in, party in hand!

Remnants of a Mariner's Tale

A sailor once lost his shoe,
Now it floats, a curious view.
Fish swim by, having a laugh,
While crabs pretend it's their craft.

With a parrot yelling, "Yo ho!",
The seagulls join in the show.
The waves dance in a jolly glee,
As jellyfish waltz quite freely!

Underneath the Glistening Surface

A clam once sought to be a star,
But ended up stuck in a jar.
Octopuses play cards at night,
While dolphins burst forth in delight.

Mermaids giggle, tails all a-flip,
Making waves in a playful trip.
The seaweed sways to their tune,
As tide pools hold a secret boon.

The Allure of the Endless Blue

A whale with a crown, quite surreal,
   Thinks he's the king of the reel.
   Fish bow down when he splashes,
But jog away from his gassy crashes!

The starfish throw a dance-off spree,
   Glittering sand, a sight to see.
   Crabs in tuxedos all parade,
  While sea cucumbers just evade.

Luminescent Dreams of the Deep

A glowing squid tells knock-knock jokes,
While shimmering snails chase after folks.
The starry night sparkles on scales,
With fish gossiping 'bout their tales.

A treasure chest filled with old hats,
Hangs tight beneath the acrobats.
Bubble parties start to unfold,
As sea beasts dance, brave and bold!

Forged in the Waters' Embrace

In a fishy suit, with a giddy grin,
I danced with the waves, let the fun begin.
Crabs snapped at my toes like they owned the place,
But I kept on wiggling, with silly grace.

Jellyfish waved like a clumsy brigade,
While I tried to surf on a soggy parade.
Seagulls squawked jokes that I just couldn't catch,
As I tumbled and giggled, what a fine match!

Canvas of the Sea's Tempest

Colors splashed like a toddler's dream,
As sea foam tickled my toes—a cream.
I painted my boat with a quirky flair,
While dolphins whispered, 'You'll need a repair!'

Waves rolled in wearing a floppy hat,
While shells chimed in, 'What's up with that?'
I lost my lunch to a sneaky sardine,
And laughed as it splashed like a scene unseen.

Whirling Colors in the Abyss

Spinning around in a whirlpool dance,
Octopuses chuckled, 'Give us a chance!'
I twirled with the tide, what a dizzying ride,
While sea stars cheered, 'Come take our side!'

A clam tried to join, but he fell on his shell,
'Just open and close, it's a real swell!'
Fish had confetti, and bubbles would pop,
As we giggled and swirled, 'Don't ever stop!'

Where Salt Meets the Earthly

On the sandy shores, I built a fine seat,
But waves crashed in, 'You'll never compete!'
With a bucket in hand and a grin like a child,
I sculpted a castle, both wobbly and wild.

The tide rolled back like a sneaky thief,
Taking my castle, leaving me in grief.
Yet laughter erupted, there's joy in the mess,
For a sandcastle's fate can be quite the jest!

Love Letters Written in Foam

Bubbles giggle, secret flows,
Tides tease all the silly toes.
Seaweed tangled, a lover's knot,
Whispers of fish, oh what a plot!

Crabs scuttle, wearing their best shoes,
Shells chuckle loudly, singing the blues.
Seagulls dive in, a tasty delight,
While dolphins dance under the moonlight.

With each wave, a new tale created,
Messages sent, but often debated.
Mermaids snicker, inked in the brine,
As messages shore up, it's dinner time!

So grab your bucket, let's write some more,
On sandy pages by the ocean's shore.
Each laugh echoes through coastal charms,
In a world where sea life always warms.

Ebbing and Flowing Reflections

A crab in a tux, how dapper he looks,
Reading the tides like old storybooks.
Seashells debate who's the best dressed,
While jellyfish twirl in their polka dot vest.

The waves bring laughter, a wild parade,
With starfish doing the limbo charade.
The tide rolls in, with a tickle and tease,
As sandcastles crumble with the greatest of ease.

Fish in tuxedos join in the fun,
Gossiping bubbles, oh what have they spun?
A sunken treasure, a sock from the shore,
"Is that what we lost?" they giggle and roar.

Ebbing and flowing, the humor does swell,
In the ocean's embrace, we all know it well.
For beneath all the waves, there's always a jest,
The humor of life, in the sea's gentle quest.

Serenity Found Within the Waves

A turtle in glasses, how wise he appears,
Counting the bubbles and sipping his beers.
Starfish grant wishes, though they've had too much,
As tides tickle dolphins with a friendly touch.

Waves bring a joy that's hard to resist,
While sea foam plays tricks and gives each fish a twist.
With a splash and a giggle, they wobble away,
In the wacky sea dance where sea creatures play.

A picnic of plankton, such a quirky feast,
With shrimp telling tales of their sushi beast.
The ocean rocks laughter, a bubbling spree,
Where serenity's found in the giggle of glee.

With each rolling wave, a chuckle resounds,
As the sea spins its yarn in whimsical grounds.
In the arms of the tide, we find joy and cheer,
For the ocean is laughing, come join us my dear!

Rhythm of the Ocean's Pulse

Waves dance around like they're at a ball,
Seagulls are DJing, having a ball.
Fish in tuxedos, they swim with flair,
Doing the conga, light as air.

Sandcastles stand, but they won't last,
As the tide rolls in, it's a slippery cast.
Crabs in bow ties, scuttle and shake,
Who knew the shore was so hard to take?

Seaweed sways to the beat of the tune,
While dolphins do flips, under the moon.
Whales hum bass lines, so deep and wide,
Creating a party, a splashy ride.

Frolicking flotsam, a sight to behold,
Teasing the seagulls, so brazen and bold.
With laughter that echoes, both loud and clear,
The rhythm here makes it hard not to cheer!

Cradle of the Deep Blue

In the cradle of waves, a whale sings low,
With a voice so deep, it sets the flow.
Octopus juggling, with a wink and a grin,
"Who knew these antics would be my win?"

Starfish lounge, calling in the sun,
Watching the antics, oh what fun!
Seashells gossip, a clique on the shore,
"Did you hear? The crabs are back for more!"

Jellyfish float with grace and style,
Dressed in their finest, they go the extra mile.
The sea's a playground, where laughter's the key,
Join the fish parties, you'll laugh with glee.

Turtles take selfies, with barnacles near,
"Just one more shot, then we'll disappear!"
Life in the blue, a whimsical spree,
Who knew such wonders were waiting for me?

Serenade of Coastal Breezes

Breezes hum softly, tunes from above,
Whistling sweet nothings, a waltz of love.
The wind plays the flutes, the sand joins the song,
As crabs make a chorus, dancing along.

Pelicans swoop, forgetting the rules,
In a comedy skit, they look like fools.
"Watch my dive now, look at me float!"
Who knew such antics made waves on a boat?

The sun sets low with a pink-orange glow,
Glowworms giggle; it's quite the show.
Sands tickle toes, as laughter erupts,
With every new wave, another joke cups.

Seashells chime in, creating a choir,
With rhythms that lift you, like never tire.
In this coastal serenade, life's a delight,
With every breeze, laughter takes flight.

Treasures Beneath the Surface

Digging for treasures in the wet, muddy sand,
"Look what I found!" yells a small, sticky hand.
Mermaids giggle, they're hiding their loot,
All eyes on the chest — it's full of old boots!

Silver spoons and a locket or two,
What a strange treasure to stumble onto!
The clams tell their tales, embellished and grand,
While sea cucumbers make quite the stand.

A treasure map leads to nothing but fun,
With laughter and giggles — the best is yet to come.
Typhoon Taco, the crab, takes the stage,
Reciting his stories with fiery rage.

What's buried beneath? Who really knows?
But the laughter above is the best kind of prose.
In the depths of the sea, life's shiny and bright,
With treasures of joy, making every night light.

Whispers of the Deep

The fish tell tales, oh what a sight,
Of crabs who dance in the moon's soft light.
A starfish claims he's a celebrity,
While the octopus laughs, 'I'm out of legibility.'

With seashells that gossip, all under the sun,
A dolphin plays tricks, oh he's such fun!
They wiggle and giggle in bubbles so bright,
Making seaweed wigs for the evening's delight.

Tides of Emotion

The waves crash down with a giggle so sweet,
As sea turtles shuffle, shuffling their feet.
A jellyfish floats, looking quite grand,
While seagulls squawk, plotting a band.

Crabs throw a party, they've parked on the shore,
With sandcastles built, they just want more!
A clam strums a guitar, what a quirky tune,
Reminding us all that we should dance soon.

Beneath the Wave's Embrace

Down where the sea cucumbers squirm and hide,
Lies a dancing anemone, full of pride.
Whales do the worm, oh what a sight,
While a pufferfish laughs, he's not feeling right.

The shrimp are all gossiping, full of tease,
As the sea urchins try to just, you know, please.
A crab chef serves up a seafood stew,
But oops! That's a sea sponge—oopsie doo!

Secrets of the Abyss

In the depths where the funny things swim and play,
A catfish sings tunes, in a jazzy way.
The anglerfish giggles with lights to show,
While the clueless goldfish just swims to and fro.

An octopus dives deep, throwing confetti around,
In a party so wild, laughter's the sound.
With mermaids who flip and swirl with the tide,
We're all waiting here for the ocean's fun ride.

Where Sea Meets Spirit

A crab in a suit, what a sight,
Dancing at sunset, oh what delight.
He twirls with a shrimp, quite the pair,
Making the seagulls pause and stare.

A fish wearing glasses, looking so wise,
Claims he's seen stars float down from the skies.
With each silly tale, the seashells just giggle,
As they listen to fishy puns and wiggle.

A dolphin on skates rolls by with a flair,
Winks at the waves, give us something to share.
The starfish applaud, flapping hands made of sand,
While the jellyfish float, a neon-bright band.

A whale with a hat leads a conga line,
With seals in tuxedos, looking so fine.
They shimmy and shake as the tide starts to sway,
Bubbling laughter makes the dolphins play!

Lullabies from the Tide

A clam sings softly, its voice smooth as cream,
    Waves lap along, joining in the dream.
    The octopus hums, rocking to and fro,
    While sea cucumbers sway to the flow.

A sea turtle croons, "Oh, don't be late!"
To the fish in a rush, who just can't wait.
Blowfish giggle, puffed up with glee,
    As they float by, "Just let it be!"

The lobsters tap dance on the sandy floor,
While whales serenade with a sonorous roar.
Their lullabies drift beneath the starry arc,
Where shadows of sea urchins brightly spark.

Anemones sway, in time with the drift,
Sending whispers of dreams, a melodic gift.
And all the small critters, tucked into the sand,
    Join the harmony, oh isn't it grand?

Reflections in the Marine Mirror

The water's a mirror, where funny fish glow,
With polka dots and stripes, ready for show.
A snapper that sneezes, a bluefin that snorts,
Flipping through bubbles, it's all sorts of sports.

A gaze at a puffer, oh my, what a sight,
Inflating in laughter, what's wrong or right?
Coral chuckles softly at jokes made in waves,
While the barnacles crack up, deep down in their caves.

A seaweed like hair, a fashion trend there,
Tangled in giggles, with nary a care.
The clownfish perform, with antics so bold,
As laughter erupts, like secrets retold.

As crabs strut around, with hats on their claws,
They boast about currents and anchor their jaws.
In the mirror of water, they twinkle and shine,
Living it up in the salty sunshine!

Mysterious Depths Unveiled

In depths of the sea where the funny things dwell,
A squid wears a bowtie, oh what a swell!
With a wink and a wiggle, he glides with a joke,
As bubbles burst forth, erupting in smoke.

A treasure chest grins, with jewels all aglow,
"Why did the pirate say 'no'?" It'll show.
"For he wanted a fish to join in his spree,
But fins are too slippery to sit at my tea!"

Sea horses prance by in their snazzy parade,
With feathers and glitter, they're perfectly made.
They flaunt through the kelp, swirling in delight,
While seahorses cheer in the soft, shimmering light.

An anglerfish chuckles, "I'm the light of this reef!"
With glow and with giggles, bringing the brief.
As mermaids all laugh 'neath the shimmering tide,
In the depths of the ocean, they cannot hide!

The Fisherman's Sonnet

With a rubber worm and a big old hat,
He baited his hook and challenged the cat.
But the fish all laughed, they wouldn't take a bite,
Claiming they were on a fast, what a sight!

The lines got tangled, as they often do,
He told them stories of struggles so true.
But the fish just giggled, splashing all around,
Saying, "We're fish, we're not here to be drowned!"

His pole went flying, a bobber took flight,
He swore he'd catch dinner if it took all night.
The seagulls cackled, swooping down like a kite,
"Your skills are so funny, this is pure delight!"

But at the end of the day, what did he find?
A shoe, an old hook, and some seaweed entwined.
He laughed to himself, with a grin ear to ear,
"Guess I'll just settle for a cold can of beer!"

Melodies of the Moonlit Bay

The moon hung low, whispering soft tunes,
While crabs danced cha-cha beneath the bright moons.
The jellyfish jiggled, throwing a light show,
As clams clapped their shells, moving to and fro.

A dolphin swam by with a wink and a flip,
He tossed out a tale from his big ocean trip.
"Swam with a mermaid, she had quite a flair,
But she stole my sandwich! Now that's just not fair!"

Fairy lights twinkled on the waves all aglow,
While turtles played limbo, putting on a show.
"It's all very nice, but have you heard my beat?
I'm the DJ tonight, feel that ocean heat!"

In the bay, laughter soared, carried by the breeze,
The critters all rocked, doing just as they please.
A party of creatures, the night was a blast,
In the moonlit bay, the memories will last.

Tracing the Shoreline of Dreams

I built a grand castle from sand and a shell,
While seagulls looked on, and began to yell.
They swooped and they squawked, demanding a snack,
But I tossed them some fries, they didn't hold back!

A kid ran past me with a bucket in tow,
Chasing the waves, trying not to go slow.
He tripped on a seaweed, fell face-first in sand,
Laughed so hard, even his dad couldn't stand!

The tides came rolling, erasing my work,
My castle collapsed, like a soggy old jerk.
But instead of a frown, I just laughed out loud,
That sand is for sculpting, not for feeling proud!

As the sun set down, we gathered for fun,
Spilling our stories, one by one.
We traced our wild dreams, as bright as the foam,
With laughter so rich, we felt right at home.

The Deep Blue's Gentle Echo

The waves whispered secrets, so silly and grand,
Making riddles and jokes—who needs a band?
A starfish named Larry was top of the show,
Said, "I'm losing my grip, can someone let me go?"

With fishes in ties and a crab acting wise,
They formed a big council, debating the skies.
"Who stole my last chip?" yelled a clam with disdain,
"Maybe it's me, I've been hungry, it's plain!"

In the depths of the water danced bubbles of cheer,
As a whale serenaded, we all swung from gear.
"Let's throw a beach bash, and invite every fin,
Or we'll be stuck clown-fishin' till we wear thin!"

So laughter erupted from the big ocean blue,
While guppies and octopi planned the hullabaloo.
With jokes and with songs echoing quite clear,
We celebrated life with a splash and a cheer!

Celestial Waters and Wandering Souls

Bubbles giggle as they rise,
Fish wear shades, oh what a surprise!
A crab walks sideways, quite refined,
While seahorses dance in a conga line.

Jellyfish float like balloons in the sky,
Starfish lounge, no reason to be shy.
The manatee rolls, with a gentle sway,
As dolphins flip, they just came to play.

A Symphony of Waves

Seashells sing with a funny tune,
A sea lion hums beneath the moon.
Octopus throws an ink-filled joke,
While surfers wipe out, creating a smoke.

Crabs in tuxedos dance on the shore,
Flipping and flapping, oh hear them roar!
The tide pulls back, a game of hide,
As waves crash in, they can't decide.

The Call of Distant Shores

Seagulls squawk out a silly song,
A beach ball bounces, meeting throngs.
A mermaid waves with a glimmering tail,
While sea cucumbers giggle and wail.

Sandcastles crumble with a splat,
A starfish exclaims, "Look at that!"
Windsurfers tumble, what a sight,
As crabs cheer on with all their might.

Journey Through Coral Dreams

Coral reefs painted with colors bright,
Fish in bow ties swim left and right.
Anemones wave like they're at a show,
As clowns swim by with a friendly glow.

Turtles text their friends, 'Meet me near!'
While a narwhal shouts, "No need to fear!"
With seaweed snacks and salty tales,
Underwater laughs, where joy never fails.

Whispered Promises in Brine

The fish all have a secret grin,
They know where all the treasures swim.
A clam whispered, "You'll never know,"
While crabs are plotting quite the show.

A dolphin laughs, he's quite the tease,
He juggles shells with effortless ease.
The seaweed dances, sways with flair,
As mermaids giggle without a care.

The octopus wears a silly hat,
While turtles chat about their spat.
The jellyfish, oh, what a sight!
Glowing softly, causing delight.

So dive in deep, let laughter ring,
In this briny realm, we'll sing and swing.
The currents twist, the bubbles burst,
In this watery world, we're surely cursed!

Eternal Blues Beneath a Wistful Sky

A crab with shades and a funky style,
Struts across the sand with a goofy smile.
The seagulls squawk in a comical tone,
While clowns in fishnets dance on their own.

The waves roll in with a splash and a dash,
Demanding attention, they make quite the splash.
A starfish winks and a blowfish pouts,
As sea turtles critique all the new routes.

Bubbles tickle and laughter ensues,
As sea creatures gossip in bright, silly hues.
The sunbeams chuckle, the tides play along,
With a shimmering echo of a sea shanty song.

Oh, the joy that the sea does bring,
A carnival ride on a whimsical fling.
Let's surf through the jests, splash through the fun,
In this blue paradise, we'll never be done!

Unraveling Stories from the Deep

Whales tout tales of ancient kings,
While mermaids strum on broken strings.
A barracuda swears he can dance,
But trips on sea grass, what a chance!

The anglerfish shines, a light in the gloom,
While sea cucumbers ponder their doom.
A clam yells, "Hey, I found a sock!"
Though all the others just laugh and mock.

Starfish spinning like a top,
While crabs play tag, they just can't stop.
The octopus juggles with eight little arms,
Each toss igniting contagious charms.

In this realm of joyful absurd,
Not a whisper of sorrow is heard.
So come explore, let the fun erupt,
In the deep sea's heart, laughter is tucked!

Where Currents Collide with Memory

The dolphins dive with a playful leap,
Recounting tales, while sea creatures sleep.
A sneaky eel winks from the gloom,
As a crab taps dance in a seashell's room.

The waves curl up with a giggle and spin,
Riding on tales held deep within.
A sunken ship hosts a party of fish,
Where sardines grant every wild wish.

The currents twist like a silly hat,
And seahorses flip as they chat and spat.
A treasure chest filled with giggles and mirth,
Reminds us of joy in our watery birth.

So, gather your laughter and ride the tide,
In this quirky place, let humor collide.
For every wave that tickles your toes,
Holds the laughter that forever flows!

Where the Waters Meet Desires

A fish in a tux, swimming in style,
Counting the waves with a cheeky smile.
He dreams of the day he'll win a big prize,
A shiny new hook, oh what a surprise!

Crabs play chess on the ocean floor,
Knocking over pieces and shouting for more.
They'll crown the best player with a grand feast,
But beware of the seagulls, they love the least!

Octopus tangoing with all of their arms,
Making a splash with their slippery charms.
With each little dance, they create quite a scene,
Underwater parties, the best ever seen!

So dive into frolics, just follow your dreams,
Where the sea is a stage for the strangest of themes.
With laughter the current, so let go with glee,
In this wacky world, we all can be free!

Lost at Sea: A Treasure Found

A pirate with map and a parrot named Lou,
Set sail for riches, but how to get through?
They stumbled on cupcakes, a sugary flood,
Now they're cleaning the deck from the frosting and mud!

Looking for gold, they found jellybeans,
In the treasure chest filled with all funny scenes.
The pirate proclaimed, 'This bounty's divine!',
As he stole a handful, and drank soda wine!

Sirens were singing with laughter and cheer,
But instead of a ship, they crashed on a pier.
"Oh, what a blunder!" the captain would say,
As they danced on the dock, in a comedic way!

So next time you chase what you think is your prize,
Remember it's fun that may be your surprise.
In the waves of mischief, let your spirit soar,
For the silliest treasures are what we adore!

Beneath the Stars, the Waters Sing

Under the stars, the waves start to hum,
With fish doing karaoke, oh what a strum!
The whales throw a party; they're all in a row,
They'll welcome the dolphins who just love the show!

A crab with a top hat leads the night's tune,
While squids play maracas, a comical swoon.
The seaweed sways gently, in sync with the beat,
As turtles tap dance in their funky little feet!

Seagulls are judges, with scorecards in beak,
Rating the moments, each funny and sleek.
As bubbles burst forth with a giggly cheer,
Who knew the night's fun would end in good beer?

So if you hear laughter beneath twinkling lights,
Just know that the ocean creates wild delights.
With song and with dance, let your heart feel the song,
In these moonlit waters, you surely belong!

Embrace of the Briny Vastness

In the briny deep where the jellyfish glide,
There's a seaweed monster who tries to hide.
But with tentacles waving, it's hard to be shy,
When the fish keep on laughing and saying, "Oh my!"

Starfish are sunbathing, with shades on their backs,
While turtles tell stories of how they got snacks.
They laugh 'til they bubble, with joy so profound,
In the embrace of the waters, true fun knows no bounds!

An octopus chef cooks up fine fishy stew,
But don't be surprised if it's got spice or two!
The critters all gather, their spirits ignite,
To feast on this banquet 'neath shimmering light!

So wade into giggles and splash in the glee,
In the briny vastness, we all can be free.
With a wink to the tides, let your worries all float,
For silliness thrives in this watery moat!

Dangers and Dreams of the Deep

A crab in a tux, he struts with flair,
stealing the spotlight, without a care.
Fish whisper secrets, they swim and they sway,
while seaweed wiggles, joining the play.

Octopus juggling, what a sight to see,
tentacles twisting, full of glee.
Beware of the shark, he's quite the tease,
offering laughter but aiming to please.

The mermaids are laughing, scales all a-glint,
as dolphins do flips, giving a hint.
Turtles wear hats, it's a costume bash,
while seagulls gossip, in a funny clash.

The deep is a circus, a riot of fun,
where every fishy tale has just begun.
So dive in with laughter, the sea's full of jokes,
as the deep plays its tricks, with its whimsical folks.

Songs of Selkie and Sea

A selkie in boots pranced over the sand,
her sealskin discarded, oh wasn't she grand?
With a boogie and wiggle, she dances in light,
stirring up mayhem on a whimsical night.

The fellowship of fish, they chant and they cheer,
while eels in top hats appear from the rear.
A starfish plays violin, quite out of tune,
inviting the crabs for a late-night cartoon.

The jellyfish glow, a disco ball's dream,
while shrimps do the conga, building a team.
They giggle and wiggle, in currents they race,
yearning for laughter, not a sad face.

So join in the revel, let loose for a while,
swim with a grin, embrace the sea's style.
With whispers of magic, the tide's a delight,
dancing with creatures, through day and through night.

Whispers of Tidal Serenades

A clam sings a ballad, all out of key,
though nobody listens, he feels quite free.
The blowfish just giggled, puffed up in place,
while otters hold hands in a watery race.

The waves tell a story of silliness near,
as sea cucumbers wobble, spreading good cheer.
A dolphin with shades, so cool and so bright,
promises laughter deep into the night.

The sea floor's a stage with critters galore,
a performance of jokes that we can't ignore.
With flounders and wrasses, how joyfully they twirl,
as the tides play their tunes in this underwater swirl.

So drift with the currents where fun is the key,
in the light of the moon, it's the place to be.
Let the whispers of tides tickle your soul,
as the sea sings its songs, making you whole.

Beneath the Waves We Wander

Beneath the blue, we giggle and glide,
with fish in bow ties, what a fun ride!
The squids write comics, the plankton create,
as the sea turtles gossip about love and fate.

Beneath the waves, where wonders are free,
a parade of sea critters, come dance with me!
Pufferfish puffing, just showing off style,
they swim with a wink and a cheeky smile.

The coral reefs chuckle with colors that play,
as they whisper big secrets in their own way.
Blowholes blow bubbles that giggle and pop,
dragging the sea floor right up to the top.

So let's splash and slosh in this underwater spree,
with every big wave bringing joy and glee.
Beneath the tide's laughter, we find our own spark,
in a world full of humor, as bright as a lark.

Cradle of the Deep Blue

In waters wide, a fishy tale,
A dolphin dance, a seaweed gale.
Crabs do tango on sandy shores,
While starfish play some silly chores.

The jellybeans swim in bright array,
With octopuses leading the ballet.
A whale serenades with goofy songs,
As the sea anemones hum along.

Seagulls gossip, squawking loud,
About the waves, they're feeling proud.
Underwater buddies hold a feast,
With shrimp and plankton, a tasty beast.

A treasure chest sings 'Open me!'
While barnacles jam in harmony.
In a splashy party, all's a joke,
In the cradle where water strokes.

Secrets Drifting on Salted Breezes

Whispers ride the salty air,
Clams gossip loudly without a care.
Seahorses giggle in a whirl,
As currents twirl and flip and swirl.

The fish all wear their fanciest fins,
While turtles splash with carefree grins.
A pirate tells tall tales of old,
While mermaids laugh and trade their gold.

Starfish play rock-paper-scissors at dawn,
While sneaky mackerels plot and yawn.
With playful waves, secrets are spread,
In the sea blue, where fun's widespread.

Even the seaweed wiggles about,
With coral giggling, without a doubt.
As tides flow in, and troubles cease,
Salted breezes bring the laughter's peace.

Rhythms of the Underwater Dream

Fish boogie down to the ocean's beat,
With kelp and plankton twirling on feet.
Dolphins leap in a bouncy show,
As crabby dancers steal the glow.

The sea cucumbers lay back in style,
While swirling waves go on for a while.
A conch shell brags with a booming sound,
His rhythm makes the whole bay astound.

Under the waves, silliness reigns,
With jellyfish floaters embracing the strains.
Even the snails try to start a band,
With tiny instruments made from sand.

The grand reef hosts a whimsical night,
As creatures all join in sheer delight.
In the currents beneath the moonbeam's glow,
Laughter floats as the rhythms grow.

Heartbeat of the Abyss

In the deep dark, bubbles start to pop,
As deep-sea fish give a rousing hop.
A squid on a skateboard zooms around,
Chasing shadows where secrets are found.

The anglerfish grins with a twinkle bright,
While lanterns flicker, casting odd light.
Cuttlefish change colors with flair,
Making a fashion show beyond compare.

The octopus spins tales of the past,
While creatures of the dark cheer and laugh.
With a wink and a wave, they call it a night,
In the heartbeat where mischief takes flight.

And who would think, in depths so profound,
That joy and fun could truly abound?
In whispers and giggles, all on display,
The abyss holds wonders, come what may.

Shadows Beneath the Surface

In the deep, where shadows play,
A crab pirouettes, a grand ballet.
Fish wear wigs made of seaweed strands,
While octopuses form rock band bands.

Seahorses gossip, tails in a twist,
Their fashion sense, one can't resist.
Starfish book club, with a saltwater sip,
Trading tales of the great ocean trip.

A turtle slips, gets stuck in sand,
"Help!" it cries, "This was not my plan!"
But the clownfish laugh, in colorful glee,
"Just wave at the sharks, they won't eat thee!"

Beneath the surface, laughter resounds,
As the ocean's quirks throw joy all around.
In this jolly realm, the antics unfold,
Waves tickle the secrets, both silly and bold.

The Siren's Call to Distant Shores

A siren sings with a fishy flair,
Tail on the rocks, with sea foam hair.
"Come join the dance!" she brightly croons,
While dolphins giggle and play the tunes.

Seagulls squawk, in a karaoke night,
Clams hum along, with all of their might.
A party beneath the shimmering tide,
Where jellyfish swirl, and turtles glide.

Anemones juggle, in a watery show,
While crabs tap dance, putting on quite a glow.
"More bubbles!" they shout, "Let's make it a blast,
Before the tide turns, let's party steadfast!"

The call of the siren, oh what a jest,
Inviting each creature to join in the fest.
Under the moonlight, with laughter ablaze,
They dance through the currents, a comical craze.

Dance of the Water's Embrace

Under the waves, where nobody cares,
Seahorses twerk, with flamboyant airs.
The fishy conga starts with a flip,
As they sway together, in a rhythmical trip.

Crabs in tuxedos, they strut with pride,
While shrimp take selfies, right by their side.
A bubble parade leads the way to the fun,
With seaweed confetti, oh what a run!

Walruses laugh, holding onto a tune,
As they dance with the rays, 'neath the bright moon.
Every creature joins in, from small to the huge,
Salty seaweed snacks the ocean's deluge.

The water's embrace, a shimmering laugh,
Riding the swells, on a whale's back raft.
Together they dance, in playful delight,
In the ocean's vastness, all is just right.

Beneath the Surface of Soulful Depths

Bubbles rise up, a giggling cheat,
As fishes blow kisses, oh so sweet.
In the depths, where silliness thrives,
Turtles wear glasses, pretending to drive.

An octopus named Larry, quite bright,
Hides all his snacks, with great delight.
"Who took my kelp?" he frantically shouts,
As the guppies swim by, laughing in bouts.

Nautilus twirls, with style it seems,
While starfish are napping, caught in big dreams.
"Hey look, a treasure!" a crab cries in glee,
Only to find it's just a lost sock spree.

In these soulful depths, comedy flows,
With jokes in the waves, how funny life goes.
The laughter resounds, in a watery sphere,
Where all of the ocean knows how to cheer.

The Dance of Tide and Time

Waves in a tango, swirl with glee,
Crabs do the cha-cha, tickled and free.
Fish in their tuxedos, spin and dive,
Clams clap their shells, feeling so alive.

Seagulls doing flips, what a sight!
Starfish are judges, giving delight.
Mermaids twirl 'round, with laughter and cheer,
Underwater disco, let's party right here!

A whale joins the fun, with a splashy move,
The sound of the ocean, it's got the groove.
With jellyfish glowing and urchins in line,
A wacky sea soirée, oh isn't it fine?

So grab your flippers, and join the parade,
For in these wild waters, all worries will fade.
Dance with the tide, let your spirit be free,
In this lively ocean, come waddle with me!

Secrets Hidden in Coral Halls

In coral castles, where shadows bloom,
Fish play hide and seek, in every room.
A clownfish giggles, peeking behind,
While an octopus tries to un-ink his mind.

Sea urchins gossip, with spiky delight,
About the new snail, who's out every night.
A pufferfish bluffing, he's quite the big shot,
With tales so tall, you'd think he's a lot!

A moray eel grins, wearing a bow tie,
He swishes and sways, as seahorses fly.
The secrets they keep, all hidden away,
Full of antics woven, in colors so gay.

When the tide comes in, oh what a show!
With everyone dancing in the water's glow.
So dive into laughter, and swirl with flair,
For in these rich halls, there's joy everywhere!

The Blue Depth's Silent Sentinels

Guardians of mischief, with shells on their backs,
Look out for trouble, and follow the tracks.
A turtle named Timmy, so wise and serene,
Chases his dreams, through algae and green.

Dolphins leap high, with a wink and a grin,
They plot silly schemes, smirking with sin.
While seaweed fluffs up, oh what a sight!
As they bubble and giggle, in the soft moonlight.

The anglerfish laughs, lighting the way,
With a bulb on his forehead, he's here to play!
Sardines in a fracas, all dart to and fro,
Caught in a whirlpool of choreographed flow.

So listen closely, to the tales that they spin,
In the blue's quiet depths, where all chuckles begin.
With each silent guard, a jest waits for you,
In this watery realm, where the laughter is true!

Oceanic Dreams on Sandy Shores

On sun-kissed sands, where sea dreams unfold,
Kids make sandcastles, both funny and bold.
A crab wears a crown, in his sandy throne,
While seagulls throw parties, never alone.

The beach ball bounces, with giggles and squeals,
Wet footprints dancing, with wobbly heels.
A starfish in sunglasses, so cool and so shy,
Flirts with the tide as it rolls by.

Kites flutter high, like fish in the air,
A sand monster emerges, without a care.
Shells painted like treasure, hidden just right,
Bring smiles and intrigue to each sunny night.

So let's build a fortune, from giggles and heaps,
Of oceanic dreams, as laughter peeps.
With tides that keep rolling, our tales will be told,
On these sandy shores, where fun never gets old!

Unveiling the Hidden Currents

Beneath the waves, where mermaids sway,
A clam named Claude has much to say.
He cracks a joke about a fish,
Who dreams of being more than a dish.

While dolphins play a game of tag,
A starfish named Stan does a brag.
He claims to dance the jig so bold,
But flops like jelly, not like gold!

An octopus may lose his key,
He'll search and search for all to see.
With eight arms waving, what a sight!
He twists and turns, day turns to night.

In seaweed forests, laughter rings,
As crabs wear hats made of shiny things.
In this world where splashes abound,
The ocean's quirks are joyfully found.

Life in Every Ripple

A fish with glasses, very droll,
Says he can read and has great soul.
But when asked for a good long look,
He flips his tail and reads a book!

The sea turtles gather for a race,
But get sidetracked, it's a slow pace.
They stop for snacks, a seaweed spread,
And nap instead, all dreams in thread.

A seagull swoops, his aim is poor,
He lands on crab, who's not at all sore.
"Why do you land on crustaceans?"
"Because you're easier than equations!"

In every wave a giggle's found,
As shells dance lightly 'round and 'round.
With shimmer and splash, joy won't conceal,
The hidden fun, oh what a reel!

Flotsam of Forgotten Tales

Washed-up shoes and half a boat,
A fish named Larry starts to gloat.
He wears the shoe, a fitting charm,
"To swim with style, now that's my aim!"

A bottle bobbing tells a tale,
Of an explorer, strong and frail.
"Adventure's great!" the note did cry,
"Until I saw a seagull fly!"

Old nets whisper secrets deep,
As crabs play hide and seek, then leap.
With laughter shared in tides so grand,
These treasures tell more than we planned.

So gather all the junk and more,
For every piece holds laughter's core.
And in the mess, true joy is found,
In tales that dance on sandy ground.

Guardians of the Marine Depths

Under the waves, a noble crew,
Of fishy knights with suits of blue.
They guard their realm, but oh, what cheer,
For they throw parties, full of beer!

A crab in armor starts to dance,
While clownfish giggle at every prance.
"Join us!" they yell, "come out and play!"
But stingrays snooze, dreaming away.

With sea cucumbers on a quest,
To find the treasure of the best.
But oh dear, they often stray,
Finding only trash, what a day!

The guardians laugh, in waves they blow,
Their joy ignites the currents' flow.
In this blue kingdom, laughter reigns,
Where silly antics wash away pains.

The Deep's Embracing Whisper

Bubbles rise, a giggling sound,
Fish wear hats when no one's around.
Octopuses dance with a cheeky flair,
Waves roll in, like they just don't care.

Crabs tap dance on the sandy floor,
Seagulls squawk, crowd for an encore.
Whales crack jokes with their mighty tails,
While starfish share their hilarious tales.

The moon snickers on the watery rim,
As jellyfish glow, looking quite dim.
Seashells whisper secrets with glee,
In a world where silliness runs free.

When Stars Dance on Water

Stars above, like disco lights,
Fish in tuxedos, ready for night flights.
The moon's a DJ, spinning tunes,
While shrimp do the cha-cha with silver spoons.

Crabs with shades strut along the shore,
Their dance moves are hard to ignore.
As dolphins giggle, leaping high,
"Catch us if you can!" they flip in the sky.

Turtles wearing sneakers run the race,
While sea cucumbers join with grace.
Anemones wave, cheering them on,
As laughter echoes until the dawn.

Ancients Beneath the Horizon

Ancient fish in old-time suits,
Debating clams over fancy roots.
Turtles recall a time gone by,
When barnacles were trendy, oh my!

Sharks with glasses read the news,
While eels gossip and share their views.
Starfish claim to have seen it all,
And boast of parties at Neptune's hall.

Coral reefs are where they meet,
For bingo night, it can't be beat!
With laughs that ripple through the deep,
The wise old fish never sleep.

Voices of the Deep: A Mysterious Ballad

Whispers float through the ocean's breeze,
Mermaids laugh, hiding behind the trees.
Crabby poets write their rhymes,
As sea turtles croon their nursery chimes.

A deep-sea creature's secret, poorly kept,
All the fish in the tank have wept.
"Why so sad?" a seahorse spied,
"We've got seaweed snacks—let's enjoy the ride!"

Echoes of jellyfish lighting the night,
They tell ghost stories, giving a fright.
With each tale spun, the laughter grows,
In the deep, where fun never slows.

Tidal Echoes of the Past

The waves brought a joke from the deep,
Shells giggled as crabs danced in heaps.
A pirate's hat floating like a lone buoy,
Yelling, "Arrr, matey! This fish is my joy!"

Seagulls squawk, plotting a food heist,
One swiped a sandwich, oh, what a Christ!
The dolphins laughed like they're in a show,
While the octopus juggled, putting on a glow.

Mermaids splashed, making a ruckus and mess,
Combing their hair, no need for finesse.
They sang with a chuckle, splashing a tune,
"Watch out for the seaweed! It's our boon!"

With a wink and a flip from a playful whale,
He signed off the party - then set sail!
The tide whispered secrets, the sand would not tell,
As laughter rolled softly, casting its spell.

Beneath the Surface, a Whisper

The fish beneath swam with a giggle,
Tickling each other's fins, oh, how they wiggle.
A shark with a grin, pretending to roar,
"Who invited the clownfish? He's quite the bore!"

Turtles tiptoed to crowdsource a trend,
"Slow is the new fast, let's all just pretend!"
With bubbles of laughter floating so light,
They plotted and schemed, oh what a sight!

Anemones swayed, taking selfies galore,
Capturing their best poses on the ocean floor.
"Watch out for the crab!" one fish yelled with cheer,
He's known to photobomb, that guy's a dear!

In the coral club, the party was on,
Dancing with currents till the break of dawn.
A conch shell DJ mixing beats on repeat,
While the sea heard their whispers, so soft and sweet.

Lanterns on the Sea's Canvas

At sunset, the jellyfish lit up like stars,
Gliding through waters—an oceanic bazaar.
Moon crabs wore hats, and they tried to boogie,
While the squids sprayed ink, feeling quite hootie.

"Is that a lighthouse or just a big blob?
Who's in charge here? It's turning into a mob!"
The fish in a frenzy, they all took a dip,
Laughing at barnacles, slick on their trip.

Lobsters in tuxes put on a parade,
Dancing on shells, what a fine charade!
They clacked and they cracked, all in good sport,
"Join our lobster ball, oh, don't be so short!"

With lanterns aglow, they painted the sea,
A canvas of chaos, delightful and free.
As laughter erupted and echoes took flight,
Ocean critters reveled in their glowing light!

Horizons of Liquid Light

The sun slipped below, painting waves orange,
While seals popped their heads, in fashion they'd forge.
"Is it sunset or breakfast?" one loudly quipped,
As the fish all laughed, their scales lightly flipped.

From the beach, they watched with snacks in hand,
A clam rolling past, didn't quite understand.
"Why are we laughing?" asked a wise old crab,
"It's just fishy business, don't lose your swag!"

Surfers splashed by on water-skimming boards,
While sea turtles taught them some clever hoards.
"Don't wipe out!" shouted one from the foam,
Or you'll need to call Dad, to bring you back home!

With horizons ablaze, all creatures would sing,
A chorus of joy, like a jubilant fling.
From dolphins to driftwood, the fun was immense,
In the shimmering sea, no need for pretense!

Echoes of Nature's Pulse

Waves whisper secrets in a salty guise,
Seagulls cry out with bubble-filled sighs.
Fish wear the latest in flashy attire,
While crabs hold a dance-off around a bonfire.

Jellyfish float like balloons on a spree,
While clams play poker, giggling with glee.
The seaweed does the cha-cha down below,
While starfish cheer them with a great big show.

Turtles in shades, looking so cool,
Shout, "Surf's up! Let's make a new rule!"
The dolphins trade jokes, splatting with grace,
In this watery kingdom, a wild, happy place.

Barnacles gossip, "Did you hear that one?"
As octopuses juggle, just having fun.
The tide rolls in like a big rubber duck,
In this giggling realm, who needs a truck?

The Language of the Forgotten Waters

Fish send tweets with bubbles of cheer,
While a lobster plays chess with a pioneer.
Octopus scribbles with ink from its brain,
Labelling seaweed as 'fancy' and 'plain.'

Mermaids take selfies, both sassy and sweet,
While crabs are busy sliding on feet.
The plankton hold parties under the moon,
With a conch-shell DJ spinning a tune.

Eels tell tall tales of treasure and fright,
While sea turtles take naps and bask in the light.
The tide flows in with a jolly old hum,
As whales join the chorus, "To infinity, come!"

Gulping down jelly, they giggle away,
In a wiggly ballet, bright colors display.
Clownfish do pranks, missing the school,
With a splash and a giggle, they're no one's fool.

Luminescence in the Shadows of the Deep

In the darkest corners where fish shine bright,
Bubbles of laughter float, a wondrous sight.
Anglerfish grinning under flickering light,
Tell tales of the mackerel's dance in the night.

Worms in the sand throw raves without fear,
As multicolored shrimp shout, "Have no fear!"
The language is laughter, a ticklish affair,
With phosphorescent blinks that light up the air.

Ghost crabs wear masks, playing hide and seek,
With a flick of their claws, they look quite unique.
Seahorses swoosh in a swirling parade,
While squids let their ink on canvas cascade.

Stalactites dripping, the pearls laugh so loud,
"We're not just pretty—let's form a crowd!"
In a prismatic glow of aquamarine,
The laughter rings out, so fresh and so keen.

A Bounty of the Briny Realm

Oh, the fish with their jokes, they tickle my gills,
Grinning wide with their bright-colored frills.
Crabs offer donuts made out of seaweed,
While shrimps craft stories with gestures of speed.

Sardines take turns on a roller-coaster,
While squids give rides on an octopus toaster.
Clownfish sing ballads, their voices so clear,
As dolphins flip pancakes, no kulk to the steer.

The sea urchins play a game of charades,
While rays do the limbo, no need for parades.
The currents all giggle, swirling with might,
In this briny bounty, everything feels right.

Barrels of laughter float on every wave,
That fill our hearts in this dance of the brave.
So, come take a plunge, feel the joy all around,
In this kingdom beneath, where laughter is found.

In the Arms of the Sea's Lullaby

The fish wear crowns of seaweed proud,
As crabs dance under waves so loud.
A dolphin slips with cheeky grace,
While seagulls compete in a catch-the-air race.

Jellyfish float with a squishy cheer,
In flip-flops, the starfish jeer.
The starfish loves to flash its star,
While clams throw shade from their little bar.

The waves giggle and tickle my toes,
While barnacles have snappy shows.
A turtle winks with a secret wink,
In this frothy fun, I hardly think.

Under water, the laughter multiplies,
As octopuses juggle with oversized pies.
With every wave and splash, a delight,
In the sea's arms, everything feels right.

Transcending Shores of Memory

We once built castles, but they washed away,
The tide giggled; 'Come, join in play!'
A sandman started wearing a hat,
While beach balls rolled, 'Hey, what of that?'

The gulls squawk secrets so loud and bold,
Chasing each other for seashells gold.
A crab plays tag, I shout, 'You cheat!'
As I trip over my own sandy feet.

Time drifts like bubbles, all shiny and bright,
Memories float in the sparkly light.
We laugh as waves crash on our sun-kissed skin,
A tangle of fun, let the day begin!

In life's ocean, we're playful and free,
With waves that tickle, just you and me.
As the sunset burns gold on the beach's floor,
Let's dance with the tides, forevermore!

The Pact of Salt and Air

In this dance of salt and breezy cheer,
The seagulls squawk a symphonic sneer.
A fish whispers jokes with watery glee,
While my beach hat flies, 'Catch me if you please!'

Clouds play tag in the bright blue sky,
While sunny rays wink, oh my, oh my!
Seashells gather, gossiping so sweet,
'Did you hear? The tide stole my seat!'

The crabs hold meetings, their claws in the air,
With instructions to dance, the sea's a big fair.
As tide pools giggle, the sea cucumbers pout,
In this salty theatre, we laugh and shout.

Dancing with jellybeans bobbing along,
Who knew the sea could host such a throng?
With every splash, a story to share,
In this contract of laughter, we're a quirky pair!

Passing Tides

The waves roll in with a ticklish kiss,
And remembrances swirl in salty bliss.
A sea sponge jokes, 'I'm not what I seem!'
While a starfish twirls, chasing the dream.

Seashells play hide and seek in the sand,
With crabs clutching treasures, so well-planned.
The dolphins giggle, leaping so high,
While I search for buried treasures nearby.

The ocean hums secrets in whispers so sweet,
As octopuses knit with their eight-legged feat.
Beach balls bounce with a bouncy cheer,
In this raucous fun, I hold the dear.

With every ebb and flow, joys arise,
A wondrous laughter beneath sunny skies.
Here in this spirit of playful delight,
Past and present swim freely in light.

Eternal Whisper

The tides tell tales as they splash and slide,
While barnacles giggle at the fun they hide.
Anemones wave like they're at a ball,
In this grand ocean, we all feel tall.

The breeze carries jokes on its breezy wings,
As sea cucumbers share their quirky flings.
Fish flaunt their scales, colors so bright,
In this watery dance, everything feels right.

The clouds drift by, floating like fluff,
'When's lunch?' asks a clam, 'I've had just enough!'
Time slips on by as seahorses prance,
In this salty circus, we'll all take a chance.

With laughter and joy, the waves intertwine,
An eternal whisper, so silly, divine.
In the water's embrace, we take a deep breath,
For in this sea, there's love past our death.

Ghosts of Wreckages Past

The old ship's ghost just wants to dance,
While rusting metal takes a chance.
With a creaky laugh and a starry wink,
It's having fun, don't you think?

Barnacles mock and barnacles cheer,
As salty tales waltz through the years.
They spin and sway on the ocean's floor,
While fish look up and ask for more.

A treasure chest filled with canned beans,
Haunting sailors in their dreams.
Each wave a joke, each swell a jest,
These wacky ghosts, they're quite the guest!

So grab your boots and join the fray,
Where shipwrecks laugh and seaweed plays.
Together they'll throw a salty bash,
While gulls glide by with a sassy flash.

Resounding Chants of the Bleating Waves

The waves sing songs like a bleating goat,
With splashes here and a foam-filled note.
Every crash is a giggle, every swell a cheer,
A symphony of laughter, let's all draw near!

Seagulls join in with a screechy tune,
While crabs tap dance under a brightening moon.
Octopuses juggle with a mischievous grin,
As the beachgoers join in and twirl with a spin.

A clam on a log thinks it's a rock star,
With a shell full of dreams and a flickering scar.
The tide rolls in with a cheeky snicker,
As fish throw parties and time gets thicker.

So next you're by the foamy shore,
Listen closely for the ocean's roar.
It's not just waves, but a carnival show,
With laughter and joy wherever you go!

A Journey Through Aquatic Depths

Dive down where the funny fish swell,
With bubble-filled giggles, they're under a spell.
A sardine parade with a comical spin,
Doing the cha-cha, let the antics begin!

Dolphins wearing sunglasses, looking chic,
Do flips and tricks, they're anything but meek.
A turtle in shades goes slow like molasses,
While jellyfish rave with their glowing sasses.

A sunken treasure turns into a ball,
As crustaceans roll out the disco ball.
Octopus DJ spins waves of delight,
With beats from the sea echoing all night.

So splash and dive into this bubbly scene,
Where laughter and joy can be heard between.
In depths so crazy, the fun never ends,
Swim with a smile, and make some new friends!

Mystical Shores of a Dreamlike Port

At the dreamlike port, where the goofballs play,
The sand tickles toes in a silly ballet.
Seashells gossip with a wink and a nod,
While flip-flops scamper, oh what a facade!

Mermaids with lemonade, laughing with glee,
Belly flop contests for all to see.
They flip through the air with a splash and a giggle,
As sea cucumbers wiggle and jiggle.

Docked are the boats with faces so bright,
They sing shanties and jokes every night.
Buoys bounce to the rhythm, a buoyant tune,
Under the watchful eye of the moon.

So wander the shores, let your worries depart,
Join the merriment, and play your part.
Where the magic is silly, and joy's always caught,
This port of laughter is the best that you've sought!

Echoes of the Coral Kingdom

In a castle made of shells,
The fish throw wild gels.
A crab gives a dance so spry,
While seahorses giggle by.

Octopuses wear hats so bright,
Suiting up for a dance tonight.
With jellybeans on their plate,
They toast to a fishy fate!

A mollusk attempts to sing,
But it sounds like a rubber band fling.
The clownfish tease with styles so bold,
While anglerfish tell tales retold.

In the kingdom of coral caves,
Everyone misbehaves.
A submarine's crashed into the scene,
And dolphins plot a prank routine.

A Symphony of Shells

On a stage made of bright sea shells,
Turtles hum, and the starfish yells.
With a wheelbarrow filled with sand,
The seaweed band is quite unplanned.

Krill join in with wings of fluke,
A marvelous and wobbly clique.
With bubbles popping everywhere,
Laughter floats upon the air.

A crab maestro waves his claws,
Yet the band just breaks the laws.
With sea cucumbers doing the twist,
They turn the starfish into a fist!

So come and join the underwater tune,
With fish acting like a buffoon.
In a concert where no one knows,
What melody will come and go!

Currents of Forgotten Memories

The fish recall a tale of yore,
Of a dolphin who lost a door.
It swam in circles, quite confused,
Chasing squid that giggled, amused.

A whale wrote a book, but it sank,
With sea turtles drawing a prank.
They swam around in a grand parade,
Laughing at the ink that sprayed.

A seaweed salad went rogue one day,
It told every fish, 'Come play!'
Goldfish strutted in shades so cool,
While eels tangled up like a fool.

Thus the tales keep flowing on,
In waves of laughter, from dusk till dawn.
For in every splash and bubbly cheer,
Are memories that still bring good cheer.

Lullabies of the Seafoam

Underneath the foamy crest,
The gulls sing out, 'You need a rest!'
With jellyfish strumming the night,
While octopuses softly take flight.

A clam plays tunes on a pearly shell,
While snails mumble, 'Oh, what the hell!'
The waves hum a sweet little song,
As the dolphins all dance along.

Anemones waltz with the breeze,
As seahorses glide with such ease.
Their laughter mixes with the tide,
In a dream where all creatures collide.

So close your eyes to the sea's soft coo,
As the night wraps around you, too.
For even in the ocean's embrace,
A funny lullaby finds its place.

Dance of the Rolling Sea

The waves are dancing, can't you see?
With jellyfish twirls, it's a jubilee!
Seagulls squawk in ridiculous glee,
As crabs do the cha-cha, oh what a spree!

Shells are tapping to a salty beat,
While sea cucumbers wiggle their feet.
A dolphin jokes, 'Hey, look at me!'
Splashing around like the life of the sea!

Starfish are lounging, taking a nap,
And barnacles glue on, what a mishap!
A fish tells a tale, "I swear it's true!"
While the ocean giggles, "Well, who would woo?"

So join the party, don't you delay,
In the waves, we'll dance all day!
Laughter and bubbles are here to stay,
In this rolling show, let's all play!

Echoes of Salt and Time

Tides whisper secrets, can you hear?
A clam says, "What's that? Pass me a beer!"
With a splash and a laugh, it's all so clear,
The barnacle chorus sings loud and near.

Starfish compose with a rhythmic twist,
While crabs hold auditions, oh what a list!
Anemones bob and never resist,
With seaweed swaying, how could you miss?

Seashells gossip like old friends do,
"Did you hear about that fish with the shoe?"
And octopuses grinning, they know it's true,
Life in the currents is quite the view!

Time flows like water, it bends and tilts,
Echoes of laughter, and all that it builds.
In the tides we'll find, our joy is distilled,
So let's raise a fin, and let's get thrilled!

Embracing the Aquatic Blue

A whale tried yoga, what a sight!
Poses in bubbles, oh what a fright!
Dolphins flip-flop, so very light,
While otters play tag, such pure delight!

With seaweed noodles twirling 'round,
Fish wear sunglasses, looking profound.
Crabs play cards on the sea floor ground,
While clams hum tunes, oh, what a sound!

Bubbles rise like champagne, hooray!
The sea creatures cheer, "It's our special day!"
With bubbles and laughter, they all sway,
In this watery world, fun's here to stay!

So if you feel blue, just take a dive,
Join in the antics, feel so alive!
In this joyful sea, the fun will thrive,
A wacky adventure where laughter will jive!

Currents of Ancient Remembrance

The sea once knew a wizard or two,
Who sailed with a parrot and wore a blue shoe!
Together they danced under the moonlight hue,
While sea turtles chuckled, "What a crew!"

Old mermaids sing songs of yesteryear,
About fishy romances with lots of cheer.
Blowfish can tell tales that bring a tear,
As the currents whisper, "Come gather near."

A crab recites poetry, quite a flair,
While lobsters applaud with claws in the air!
Coral reefs shimmer, all colors to share,
In the halls of the ocean, joy's everywhere!

So dip your toes in, feel the fun flow,
For the ocean's laughter will always glow.
In the surf and the tides, let good vibes grow,
With echoes of stories, and memories so slow!

Waves That Hold Our Secrets

In a sea of giggles, we splash and play,
Finding lost treasures that float away.
Seagulls squawk jokes, oh what a sight,
While starfish dance under the moonlight.

Crabs don tiny hats, holding court on the sand,
They chuckle at waves, thinking they're grand.
Octopuses juggle, what a comical show,
While fishes swim by in a synchronized row.

Shells tell tales of a grand marine life,
Where dolphins have parties, and seahorses strife.
Seaweed winks, it's a hairy affair,
As we all get soaked in the salty cool air.

So join in the laughter, don't drift away,
For the sea's full of secrets, come out to play.
With each joyful wave, let worries be gone,
In this sea of fun, we all just belong.

The Salted Sanctuary

In a hut made of driftwood, we sip on our drinks,
With a splash of lime and the ocean's sweet winks.
Tarantulas prance while we bake in the sun,
Our toes dance with crabs - oh, this is such fun!

The waves whisper secrets, while gulls laugh aloud,
As we play chess with clams, we're feeling quite proud.
A turtle in shades rides a surfboard with flair,
He winks at the jellyfish floating in air.

The breeze carries laughter, like wild ocean songs,
As mermaids compose the most humorous wrongs.
Fish jump in rhythm, how silly they seem,
In this sanctuary spun from a salty daydream.

So come, grab a conch, let the laughter commence,
For the ocean's our playground, that's simply immense.
With a sprinkle of joy and a twist of delight,
We'll ride the tides all day and night.

Tides of Time and Memory

Time tickles the shore, like a playful old friend,
Each wave a reminder that we cannot bend.
Sand castles crumble, yet memories thrive,
As crabs steal our lunch, oh, how we survive!

The sun's giggle echoes as gulls do their dance,
While fish wear top hats for a saltwater prance.
Oysters throw shade at the sun's silly glow,
As we wrestle with tides that ebb to and fro.

Seashells chuckle softly, sharing tales from the deep,
Of underwater picnics where sea monsters creep.
Each tide that rolls in brings a new dose of fun,
Funny faces in the foam—oh, this is just begun!

So let's ride each wave of this whimsical jest,
In laughter and joy, we are truly blessed.
With the tide as our guide, let's skip through the day,
In the rhythm of life, let our worries float away.

Reflections of the Nautical Soul

In water mirrors, we spot our silly glee,
As fishy reflections start giggling at me.
The dolphins send selfies to everyone near,
While we laugh at the seaweed stuck in our hair.

The submarines dance in a flamboyant parade,
While whales hum tunes like a quirky charade.
A sea turtle's fashion just never goes wrong,
In polka dots, stripes—always wavy and strong!

The sand whispers secrets that tickle our feet,
With tides that bring laughter, oh, isn't it neat?
A crab in a bowtie winks at us sly,
While clams crack up, thinking we're rather spry.

So gather your friends, let the fun sail away,
In the ocean's reflection, let's dance and sway.
With laughter as our compass, we'll drift with the flow,
In this realm of the sea, let our joys overflow.

www.ingramcontent.com/pod-product-compliance
Lightning Source LLC
Chambersburg PA
CBHW072216070526
44585CB00015B/1360